COUNTRY
Soups

Publications International, Ltd.

Favorite Brand Name Recipes at www.fbnr.com

ISBN-13: 978-1-4127-5437-8
ISBN-10: 1-4127-5437-2

Manufactured in China.

8 7 6 5 4 3 2 1

Microwave Cooking: Microwave ovens vary in wattage. Use the cooking times as guidelines and check for doneness before adding more time.

Preparation/Cooking Times: Preparation times are based on the approximate amount of time required to assemble the recipe before cooking, baking, chilling or serving. These times include preparation steps such as measuring, chopping and mixing. The fact that some preparations and cooking can be done simultaneously is taken into account. Preparation of optional ingredients and serving suggestions is not included.

Table of Contents

***

Beef & Pork -------------------------------- 6

Chicken & Turkey -------------------------- 20

Vegetables & Grains ----------------------- 36

Beans & Legumes --------------------------- 56

Chowders & Bisques ------------------------ 66

Chilis & Gumbos --------------------------- 78

Acknowledgments --------------------------- 91

Index ------------------------------------- 92

Beef & Pork

***

Beefy Broccoli & Cheese Soup

  2 cups chicken broth

  1 package (10 ounces) frozen chopped broccoli, thawed

  ¼ cup chopped onion

  ¼ pound ground beef

  1 cup milk

  2 tablespoons all-purpose flour

  1 cup (4 ounces) shredded sharp Cheddar cheese

1½ teaspoons chopped fresh oregano *or* ½ teaspoon dried oregano

    Salt and black pepper

    Hot pepper sauce

1. Bring broth to a boil in medium saucepan. Add broccoli and onion; cook 5 minutes or until broccoli is tender.

2. Meanwhile, brown beef in small skillet 6 to 8 minutes over medium-high heat, stirring to break up meat. Drain fat. Gradually add milk to flour in small bowl, mixing until well blended. Add milk mixture and beef to broth mixture; cook, stirring constantly, until mixture is thickened and bubbly.

3. Add cheese and oregano; stir until cheese is melted. Season to taste with salt, black pepper and hot pepper sauce. *Makes 4 servings*

Ham, Potato & Cabbage Soup

1 tablespoon vegetable oil

1 large sweet onion, chopped (about 2 cups)

1 clove garlic, minced

6 cups SWANSON® Chicken Broth (Regular, Natural Goodness™
    or Certified Organic)

¼ teaspoon ground black pepper

3 cups shredded cabbage

1 large potato, diced (about 2 cups)

½ of an 8-ounce cooked ham steak, cut into 2-inch-long strips
    (about 1 cup)

2 tablespoons chopped fresh parsley

1 teaspoon caraway seed (optional)

1. Heat the oil in a 6-quart saucepot over medium-high heat. Add the onion and garlic and cook for 3 minutes or until tender.

2. Stir in the broth, black pepper, cabbage, potato and ham. Heat to a boil. Reduce the heat to medium-low. Cover and cook for 20 minutes or until the potato is tender.

3. Stir in the parsley and caraway seed, if desired.   *Makes 6 servings*

Kitchen Tip: A small head of cabbage, about 1 pound, will be enough for the amount of cabbage needed for this soup.

Prep Time: 15 minutes
Cook Time: 30 minutes

Ham, Potato & Cabbage Soup

Grandma Ruth's Minestrone

1 pound ground beef

1 can (about 15 ounces) red beans or kidney beans, rinsed and drained

1 package (16 ounces) frozen mixed vegetables

2 cans (8 ounces each) tomato sauce

1 can (about 14 ounces) diced tomatoes

2 cups shredded cabbage

1 cup chopped onion

1 cup chopped celery

½ cup chopped fresh parsley

1 tablespoon dried basil

1 tablespoon Italian seasoning

1 teaspoon salt

1 teaspoon black pepper

1 cup cooked macaroni

Slow Cooker Directions

1. Brown beef in large skillet over medium-high heat, stirring to break up meat. Drain fat.

2. Place beef and all remaining ingredients except macaroni in slow cooker; stir to blend. Cover; cook on LOW 6 hours.

3. Stir in macaroni. Cover; cook on HIGH 30 minutes.   *Makes 4 servings*

Tip

Browning meat and poultry before cooking them in a slow cooker is not necessary, but it can enhance the flavor and appearance of the finished dish. Browning also helps reduce the fat, provided that you drain off any excess fat before transferring the meat to the slow cooker.

Kansas City Steak Soup

½ pound ground beef

1 cup chopped onion

3 cups frozen mixed vegetables

2 cups water

1 can (about 14 ounces) stewed tomatoes, undrained

1 cup sliced celery

1 beef bouillon cube

½ to 1 teaspoon black pepper

1 can (about 14 ounces) reduced-sodium beef broth

½ cup all-purpose flour

1. Spray large saucepan or Dutch oven with nonstick cooking spray. Brown beef over medium-high heat 6 to 8 minutes, stirring to break up meat. Drain fat.

2. Add vegetables, water, tomatoes with juice, celery, bouillon cube and pepper; bring to a boil. Whisk broth and flour in small bowl until smooth; add to beef mixture, stirring constantly. Return to a boil. Reduce heat to low. Cover and simmer 15 minutes, stirring frequently.   *Makes 6 servings*

Meatball & Pasta Soup

2 cans (14½ ounces each) chicken broth

4 cups water

1 can (15 ounces) crushed tomatoes

1 package (15 ounces) frozen precooked Italian style meatballs, not in sauce

1 envelope LIPTON® RECIPE SECRETS® Onion Soup Mix

½ teaspoon LAWRY'S® Garlic Powder with Parsley

1 cup uncooked mini pasta (such as conchigliette or ditalini)

4 cups fresh baby spinach leaves

1. In 6-quart saucepan, bring broth, water, crushed tomatoes, meatballs, soup mix and Garlic Powder with Parsley to a boil over medium-high heat.

2. Add pasta and cook 5 minutes or until pasta is almost tender. Stir in spinach. Reduce heat to medium and simmer uncovered, 2 minutes or until spinach is wilted and pasta is tender. Serve, if desired, with Parmesan cheese.
Makes 8 servings

Kansas City Steak Soup

Homestyle Ham & Bean Soup

1 large yellow onion, chopped
1 cup sliced carrots
1 cup sliced celery
2 cloves minced garlic
2 tablespoons olive or vegetable oil
6 cups chicken broth
2 (15-ounce) cans Great Northern beans
2 (5-ounce) cans HORMEL® chunk ham
¼ teaspoon ground white pepper
¼ teaspoon dried thyme leaves
    Chopped fresh parsley (optional)

In 5-quart saucepan, sauté onion, carrots, celery and garlic in oil until golden, about 5 to 7 minutes. Add chicken broth, beans, ham, white pepper and thyme. Cook and stir until warmed through, about 15 minutes. Ladle soup into warm bowls and serve. If desired, top with chopped fresh parsley.

Makes 8 servings

Serving Suggestion: To add extra kick to your ham and bean soup, serve it with hot pepper sauce on the side.

Lasagna-Style Soup

1 large yellow onion, chopped
2 green and/or red bell peppers, chopped
2 cloves garlic, minced
1 pound lean ground beef
½ pound ground Italian sausage
8 cups water
9 cubes HERB-OX® beef flavored bouillon
2 (14½-ounce) cans chopped tomatoes with basil, garlic and oregano
8 ounces campanelle pasta or 8 ounces malfada (mini-lasagna) pasta, broken into pieces
1 teaspoon Italian seasoning
    Salt and pepper, to taste
    Ricotta and shredded Parmesan cheese

In large stockpot over medium-high heat, sauté onion, bell peppers, garlic, ground beef and Italian sausage until meat is cooked through, about 15 minutes; drain any excess fat. Add water, bouillon, tomatoes, pasta and Italian seasoning. Bring mixture to a boil. Reduce heat and simmer until pasta is cooked through, about 10 to 12 minutes. Season soup with salt and pepper. If desired, top with ricotta and Parmesan cheese.   *Makes 14 cups*

1-2-3 Steak Soup

    1 pound boneless beef sirloin steak, cut into 1-inch cubes
    1 tablespoon vegetable oil
    ½ pound sliced mushrooms (about 2½ cups)
    2 cups *French's®* French Fried Onions, divided
    1 package (16 ounces) frozen vegetables for stew (potatoes, carrots, celery and pearl onions)
    2 cans (14½ ounces each) beef broth
    1 can (8 ounces) tomato sauce
    1 tablespoon *French's®* Worcestershire Sauce
      Garnish: chopped parsley (optional)

1. Cook beef in hot oil in large saucepan over medium heat until browned, stirring frequently. Remove beef from pan; set aside.

2. Sauté mushrooms and ⅔ *cup* French Fried Onions in drippings in same pan over medium heat until golden, stirring occasionally. Stir in vegetables, broth, tomato sauce and Worcestershire. Return beef to pan.

3. Heat to a boil over high heat; reduce heat to low. Cover and simmer 20 minutes or until vegetables are tender, stirring occasionally. Spoon soup into serving bowls; top with remaining onions. Garnish with chopped parsley, if desired.   *Makes 8 servings*

Prep Time: 5 minutes
Cook Time: 30 minutes

Beef, Lentil and Onion Soup

  1 tablespoon olive or vegetable oil
¾ pound beef stew meat (1-inch pieces)
  2 cups chopped carrots
  1 cup sliced celery
  1 cup uncooked lentils
  2 teaspoons dried thyme
¼ teaspoon black pepper
⅛ teaspoon salt
3¼ cups water
  1 can (10¾ ounces) condensed French onion soup, undiluted

Slow Cooker Directions

1. Heat oil in large skillet over medium-high heat. Add beef; cook until browned on all sides.

2. Place carrots, celery and lentils in 3½- to 4-quart slow cooker. Top with beef; sprinkle with thyme, pepper and salt. Pour water and soup over mixture. Cover; cook on LOW 7 to 8 hours or HIGH 3½ to 4 hours or until meat and lentils are tender.

Makes 4 servings

Tip

Always sort through lentils before using them, discarding any debris or blemished lentils, and rinse in a colander under cold running water. Unlike dried beans, lentils do not need to be soaked before cooking, so they are a very versatile addition to soups and stews.

Beef and Beet Borscht

2 cans (15 ounces each) julienned beets
1 cup buttermilk
⅛ teaspoon black pepper
⅛ teaspoon ground cloves
1 cup reduced-sodium beef broth
4 ounces thinly sliced deli roast beef, cut into short thin strips
¼ cup sour cream

1. Drain beets, reserving 1 cup liquid. Pour 1 can beets into food processor; process until finely chopped. Add buttermilk, pepper and cloves; process until smooth. Transfer to medium bowl.

2. Stir in remaining beets, broth, reserved beet liquid and roast beef. Cover and chill at least 2 hours or up to 24 hours. Top with sour cream just before serving. *Makes 4 servings*

Kielbasa & Cabbage Soup

1 pound Polish kielbasa, cut into ½-inch cubes
1 package (16 ounces) coleslaw mix (shredded green cabbage and carrots)
3 cans (14½ ounces each) beef broth
1 can (12 ounces) beer or nonalcoholic malt beverage
1 cup water
½ teaspoon caraway seeds
2 cups *French's*® French Fried Onions, divided
Garnish: fresh dill sprigs (optional)

1. Coat 5-quart pot or Dutch oven with nonstick cooking spray. Cook kielbasa over medium-high heat about 5 minutes or until browned. Add coleslaw mix; sauté until tender.

2. Add broth, beer, water, caraway seeds and *1 cup* French Fried Onions; bring to a boil over medium-high heat. Reduce heat to low. Simmer, uncovered, 10 minutes to blend flavors. Spoon soup into serving bowls; top with remaining onions. Garnish with fresh dill sprigs, if desired. *Makes 8 servings*

Beef and Beet Borscht

Chicken & Turkey
* * *

Spaghetti Soup

2 tablespoons vegetable oil

½ pound skinless, boneless chicken breast halves, cut into cubes

1 medium onion, chopped (about ½ cup)

1 large carrot, chopped (about ½ cup)

1 stalk celery, finely chopped (about ½ cup)

2 cloves garlic, minced

4 cups SWANSON® Chicken Broth (Regular, Natural Goodness™ *or* Certified Organic)

1 can (10¾ ounces) CAMPBELL'S® Condensed Tomato Soup (Regular, Healthy Request® *or* 25% Less Sodium)

1 cup water

3 ounces uncooked spaghetti, broken into 1-inch pieces

2 tablespoons chopped fresh parsley (optional)

1. Heat **1 tablespoon** oil in a 6-quart saucepot over medium-high heat. Add the chicken and cook until well browned, stirring often. Remove the chicken from the saucepot.

2. Add the remaining oil to the saucepot and heat over medium heat. Add the onion and cook for 1 minute. Add the carrot and cook for 1 minute. Add the celery and garlic and cook for 1 minute.

3. Stir in the broth, soup and water. Heat to a boil. Stir in the pasta. Cook for 10 minutes or until the pasta is tender. Stir in the chicken and parsley, if desired, and cook until the mixture is hot and bubbling.

Makes 4 servings

Prep Time: 15 minutes
Cook Time: 30 minutes

Country Turkey and Veggie Soup

2 tablespoons butter, divided
8 ounces sliced mushrooms
½ cup chopped onion
½ cup thinly sliced celery
1 medium carrot, thinly sliced
1 medium red bell pepper, chopped
½ teaspoon dried thyme
4 cups chicken or turkey broth
4 ounces uncooked egg noodles
2 cups chopped cooked turkey
1 cup half-and-half
½ cup frozen peas, thawed
¾ teaspoon salt

Slow Cooker Directions

1. Melt 1 tablespoon butter in large nonstick skillet over medium-high heat. Add mushrooms and onion; cook and stir 4 minutes or until onion is translucent.

2. Spray 3-quart slow cooker with nonstick cooking spray. Add mushroom mixture, celery, carrot, bell pepper, thyme and broth. Cover; cook on HIGH 2½ hours.

3. Add noodles and turkey to slow cooker. Cover; cook on HIGH 20 minutes. Stir in half-and-half, peas, remaining 1 tablespoon butter and salt; cook until heated through.
Makes 8 servings

Country Turkey and Veggie Soup

Chicken & Herb Dumplings

2 pounds skinless, boneless chicken breasts and/or thighs, cut into
   1-inch pieces

5 medium carrots, cut into 1-inch pieces (about 2½ cups)

4 stalks celery, cut into 1-inch pieces (about 2 cups)

2 cups frozen whole kernel corn

3½ cups SWANSON® Chicken Broth (Regular, Natural Goodness™
   or Certified Organic)

¼ teaspoon ground black pepper

¼ cup all-purpose flour

½ cup water

2 cups all-purpose baking mix

⅔ cup milk

1 tablespoon chopped fresh rosemary leaves or 1 teaspoon dried
   rosemary leaves, crushed

1. Stir the chicken, carrots, celery, corn, broth and black pepper in a 6-quart slow cooker.

2. Cover and cook on LOW for 7 to 8 hours* or until the chicken is cooked through.

3. Stir the flour and water in a small bowl until the mixture is smooth. Stir the flour mixture in the cooker. Turn the heat to HIGH. Cover and cook for 5 minutes or until the mixture boils and thickens.

4. Stir the baking mix, milk and rosemary in a medium bowl. Drop the batter by rounded tablespoonfuls over the chicken mixture. Tilt the lid to vent and cook on HIGH for 40 minutes or until the dumplings are cooked in the center.
                                                              Makes 8 servings

Or on HIGH for 4 to 5 hours.

Kitchen Tip: Leaving the lid slightly ajar prevents condensation from dripping onto the dumplings during cooking.

Prep Time: 20 minutes
Cook Time: 7 hours, 45 minutes

Chicken and Wild Rice Soup

½ cup uncooked wild rice

5 cups chicken broth, divided

¼ cup (½ stick) butter

1 large carrot, sliced

1 medium onion, chopped

2 stalks celery, chopped

¼ pound fresh mushrooms, sliced

2 tablespoons all-purpose flour

¼ teaspoon salt

¼ teaspoon white pepper

1½ cups chopped cooked chicken

¼ cup dry sherry

1. Rinse rice thoroughly in fine strainer under cold running water; drain.

2. Combine 2½ cups broth and rice in small saucepan; bring to a boil over medium-high heat. Reduce heat to low; cover and simmer 1 hour or until rice is tender. Drain; set aside.

3. Melt butter in large saucepan over medium heat. Add carrot; cook and stir 3 minutes. Add onion, celery and mushrooms; cook and stir 3 to 4 minutes or until vegetables are tender. Remove from heat; whisk in flour, salt and pepper until smooth.

4. Gradually stir in remaining 2½ cups broth. Bring to a boil over medium heat; cook and stir 1 minute or until thickened. Stir in chicken and sherry. Reduce heat to low; simmer, uncovered, 3 minutes or until heated through.

5. Spoon ¼ cup rice into each serving bowl. Ladle soup over rice.

Makes 4 to 6 servings

Shaker Chicken and Noodle Soup

13 cups chicken broth, divided
¼ cup dry vermouth
¼ cup (½ stick) butter
1 cup whipping cream
1 package (12 ounces) uncooked egg noodles
1 cup thinly sliced celery
1½ cups water
¾ cup all-purpose flour
2 cups diced cooked chicken
   Salt and black pepper
¼ cup finely chopped fresh parsley (optional)

1. Combine 1 cup broth, vermouth and butter in small saucepan; bring to a boil over high heat. Boil 15 to 20 minutes or until liquid is reduced to ¼ cup and has syrupy consistency. Stir in cream; set aside.

2. Bring remaining 12 cups broth to a boil in large saucepan or Dutch oven. Add noodles and celery; cook until noodles are just tender.

3. Combine water and flour in medium bowl until smooth. Stir into broth mixture. Boil 2 minutes, stirring constantly.

4. Stir in reserved cream mixture until blended. Add chicken; season to taste with salt and pepper. Heat just until soup is hot. *Do not boil.* Sprinkle with parsley, if desired.

Makes 12 servings

Turkey and Rice Soup

2 cups JENNIE-O TURKEY STORE® Turkey, cooked, cut in bite-size pieces
8 cups water
2 stalks celery, sliced
1 onion, chopped
3 chicken bouillon cubes
¼ teaspoon poultry seasoning
1 bay leaf
¾ cup uncooked long-grain rice
2 carrots, peeled and sliced

Combine first 7 ingredients in 2½-quart saucepan. Bring to a boil; cover, reduce heat and simmer 40 minutes. Add rice and carrots; cover and simmer additional 20 minutes or until rice is tender. Remove bay leaf before serving.

Makes 4 servings

Prep Time: 30 minutes
Cook Time: 1 hour

Chunky Chicken Vegetable Soup

  1 teaspoon vegetable oil
½ pound boneless skinless chicken breasts, cut into ½-inch cubes
  1 can (14½ ounces) chicken broth
  2 cups water
  2 cups assorted cut-up vegetables (sliced carrots, broccoli florets, chopped red bell pepper)*
  1 packet Italian salad dressing and recipe mix
  1 cup MINUTE® White Rice, uncooked
  2 tablespoons chopped fresh parsley

Or substitute 1 package (10 ounces) frozen mixed vegetables, thawed.

Heat oil in large saucepan over medium-high heat. Add chicken; cook and stir until browned. Add broth, water, vegetables and salad dressing mix. Bring to a boil. Reduce heat to low; cover. Simmer 5 minutes. Stir in rice and parsley; cover. Remove from heat. Let stand 5 minutes. *Makes 4 servings*

Rich and Hearty Drumstick Soup

2 turkey drumsticks (about 1¾ pounds total)

3 carrots, peeled and sliced

3 stalks celery, thinly sliced

1 onion, chopped

2 cloves garlic, minced

1 teaspoon poultry seasoning

1 container (32 ounces) chicken broth

3 cups water

8 ounces uncooked egg noodles

⅓ cup chopped parsley

　　Salt and black pepper

Slow Cooker Directions

1. Spray 5-quart slow cooker with nonstick cooking spray. Add turkey, carrots, celery, onion, garlic and poultry seasoning to slow cooker; pour in broth and water. Cover; cook on HIGH 5 hours or until meat is falling off bones.

2. Remove turkey; set aside. Add noodles to slow cooker. Cover; cook 30 minutes more or until noodles are tender. Meanwhile, remove and discard skin and bones from turkey; shred meat.

3. Return turkey to slow cooker. Stir in parsley. Season to taste with salt and pepper.

Makes 8 servings

Chicken Tortellini Soup

2 tablespoons olive oil

4 boneless, skinless chicken breast halves, cut into bite-size pieces

2 ribs celery, cut into ¼-inch slices

1 medium carrot, cut into ¼-inch slices

1 medium onion, diced

2 cloves garlic, minced

6 cups canned or packaged fat-free, reduced-sodium chicken broth

2 cups water

1 can (14½ ounces) diced tomatoes

2 small zucchini, halved lengthwise, cut into ½-inch slices

½ teaspoon pepper

½ teaspoon Italian seasoning

1 package (9 ounces) plain or spinach cheese-filled tortellini

Salt to taste

Freshly grated Parmesan cheese

In 5-quart saucepan or Dutch oven, heat oil to medium-high temperature. Add chicken, celery, carrot, onion and garlic; cook, stirring, about 8 minutes or until chicken is lightly browned and vegetables are tender-crisp. Add broth, water, tomatoes, zucchini, pepper and Italian seasoning. Heat to boiling; reduce heat, cover and cook 7 minutes. Return to boiling, add tortellini and cook 7 minutes or until tortellini are done. Season with salt. Serve in individual bowls; top with Parmesan cheese. *Makes 6 servings*

Favorite recipe from ***Delmarva Poultry Industry, Inc.***

Creamy Chicken Tortilla Soup

   1 small red pepper, chopped (about ½ cup)
   1 small tomato, diced (about ½ cup)
   1 can (8¾ ounces) whole kernel corn, drained
  ½ pound skinless, boneless chicken breasts, cut into ½-inch pieces
   1 can (10¾ ounces) CAMPBELL'S® Condensed Cream of Chicken Soup
      (Regular *or* 98% Fat Free)
1½ cups water
  1 teaspoon ground cumin
  ½ teaspoon ground coriander
  ½ teaspoon garlic powder
  ½ teaspoon chili powder
  1 can (about 4 ounces) chopped green chiles
  ¼ teaspoon chopped jalapeño pepper (optional)
  2 corn tortillas (6-inch), cut into strips
  ½ cup shredded Cheddar cheese
  ¼ cup chopped fresh cilantro leaves

1. Stir the pepper, tomato, corn and chicken in a 3½-quart slow cooker.

2. Stir the soup, water, cumin, coriander, garlic powder, chili powder, chiles and jalapeño pepper, if desired, in a small bowl. Pour over the chicken mixture.

3. Cover and cook on LOW for 4 to 5 hours* or until the chicken is cooked through.

4. Stir in the tortillas, cheese and cilantro. Cover and cook for 30 minutes. Serve with additional cheese, if desired.   *Makes 4 servings*

Or on HIGH for 2 to 2½ hours.

Prep Time: 10 minutes
Cook Time: 4 hours

Vegetables & Grains

* * *

Cheesy Spinach Soup

1 tablespoon soft reduced calorie margarine
¼ cup chopped onions
2 cups fat-free milk
½ pound (8 ounces) VELVEETA® Made With 2% Milk Reduced Fat
    Pasteurized Prepared Cheese Product, cut into ½-inch cubes
1 package (10 ounces) frozen chopped spinach, cooked, well drained
⅛ teaspoon ground nutmeg
    Dash pepper

Melt margarine in medium saucepan on medium heat. Add onions; cook and stir until tender.

Add remaining ingredients; cook on low heat until VELVEETA® is melted and soup is heated through, stirring occasionally.

Makes 4 servings (about 1 cup each)

Substitution: Prepare as directed, substituting frozen chopped broccoli for the spinach.

Microwave Directions: Microwave onions and margarine in medium microwavable bowl on high 30 seconds to 1 minute or until onions are tender. Stir in remaining ingredients. Microwave 6 to 8 minutes or until VELVEETA® is completely melted and soup is heated through, stirring every 3 minutes.

Prep Time: 15 minutes
Total Time: 25 minutes

Greens, White Bean and Barley Soup

2 tablespoons olive oil

3 carrots, diced

1½ cups chopped onions

2 cloves garlic, minced

1½ cups sliced mushrooms

6 cups vegetable broth

2 cups cooked barley

1 can (about 15 ounces) Great Northern beans, rinsed and drained

2 bay leaves

1 teaspoon sugar

1 teaspoon dried thyme

7 cups chopped stemmed collard greens (about 24 ounces)

1 tablespoon white wine vinegar

Hot pepper sauce

Red bell pepper strips (optional)

1. Heat oil in large saucepan or Dutch oven over medium heat. Add carrots, onions and garlic; cook and stir 3 minutes. Add mushrooms; cook and stir 5 minutes or until carrots are tender.

2. Add broth, barley, beans, bay leaves, sugar and thyme; bring to a boil over high heat. Reduce heat; cover and simmer 5 minutes. Add greens; simmer 10 minutes.

3. Remove and discard bay leaves. Stir in vinegar; season to taste with pepper sauce. Garnish with bell pepper strips. *Makes 8 servings*

Tomato Soup

1 tablespoon vegetable oil
1 cup chopped onion
2 cloves garlic, coarsely chopped
½ cup chopped carrot
¼ cup chopped celery
2 cans (28 ounces each) crushed tomatoes in tomato purée
3½ cups chicken broth*
1 tablespoon Worcestershire sauce
½ teaspoon salt
½ teaspoon dried thyme
¼ to ½ teaspoon black pepper
2 to 4 drops hot pepper sauce

*Or substitute 2 cans (10½ ounces each) condensed chicken broth and 1 cup water for 3½ cups chicken broth.

1. Heat oil in large saucepan or Dutch oven over medium-high heat. Add onion and garlic; cook and stir 1 to 2 minutes or until onion is soft. Add carrot and celery; cook 7 to 9 minutes or until tender, stirring frequently.

2. Stir in tomatoes, broth, Worcestershire sauce, salt, thyme, pepper and pepper sauce. Reduce heat to low; cover and simmer 20 minutes, stirring frequently.

3. For smoother soup, remove from heat; let cool about 10 minutes. Process soup in small batches in food processor or blender until smooth. Return soup to saucepan; simmer 3 to 5 minutes or until heated through.

Makes 6 servings

Twice-Baked Potato Soup

6 large baking potatoes, scrubbed and pricked with a fork
2 tablespoons butter
1 small sweet onion, finely chopped (about ½ cup)
5 cups SWANSON® Chicken Broth (Regular, Natural Goodness™
    ***or* Certified Organic)**
¼ cup light cream
1 tablespoon chopped fresh chives
    Potato Toppers

1. Heat the oven to 425°F. Arrange the potatoes on a rack and bake for 30 minutes or until tender. Place the potatoes in a bowl with a lid and let steam. Remove the skin and mash the pulp.

2. Heat the butter in a 3-quart saucepan. Add the onion and cook until tender. Add the broth and **5 cups** of the potato pulp.

3. Place ⅓ of the broth mixture into an electric blender or food processor container. Cover and blend until smooth. Place in a medium bowl. Repeat the blending process with the remaining broth mixture. Return all of the puréed mixture to the saucepan. Stir in the cream and chives and cook for 5 minutes more. Season to taste.

4. Place ¼ **cup** of the remaining pulp mixture in each of 8 serving bowls. Divide the broth mixture among the bowls. Serve with one or more Potato Toppers.   *Makes 8 servings*

Potato Toppers: Cooked crumbled bacon, shredded Cheddar cheese **and/or** sour cream.

Time-Saving Tip: Microwave the potatoes on HIGH for 10 to 12 minutes or until fork-tender.

Prep Time: 10 minutes
Cook Time: 45 minutes

Hearty Mushroom Barley Soup

  1 tablespoon olive oil

  2 cups chopped onions

  1 cup thinly sliced carrots

  2 cans (about 14 ounces each) reduced-sodium chicken broth

12 ounces sliced mushrooms

  1 can (10¾ ounces) cream of mushroom soup, undiluted

  ½ cup uncooked quick-cooking barley

  1 teaspoon Worcestershire sauce

  ½ teaspoon dried thyme

  ¼ cup finely chopped green onions

  ¼ teaspoon salt

  ¼ teaspoon black pepper

1. Heat oil in large saucepan over medium-high heat. Add onions; cook and stir 8 minutes or until onions just begin to turn golden. Add carrots; cook and stir 2 minutes.

2. Add broth, mushrooms, soup, barley, Worcestershire sauce and thyme; bring to a boil over high heat. Reduce heat; cover and simmer 15 minutes, stirring occasionally. Stir in green onions, salt and pepper.

Makes 4 servings

Sweet Potato & Pecan Soup

2 tablespoons unsalted butter

1 large sweet onion, chopped (about 2 cups)

4 cloves garlic, minced

6 cups SWANSON® Vegetable Broth (Regular *or* Certified Organic)

2 bay leaves

3 large sweet potatoes, peeled and cut into cubes (about 6 cups)

¼ teaspoon ground black pepper

1 cup heavy cream, divided

3 tablespoons thinly sliced fresh chives

1 cup pecans, toasted

1. Heat the butter in a 6-quart saucepot over medium heat. Add the onion and garlic and cook until the onions are tender. Add the broth, bay leaves, potatoes and black pepper. Heat to a boil. Reduce the heat to low. Cover and cook for 20 minutes or until the potatoes are tender. Discard the bay leaves. Add ½ **cup** of the cream and heat through.

2. Place ⅓ of the broth mixture in an electric blender or food processor container. Cover and blend until smooth. Pour the mixture into a large bowl. Repeat the blending process twice more with the remaining broth mixture. Return all of the puréed mixture to the saucepot. Cook over medium heat for 5 minutes or until hot. Season to taste.

3. Prepare the *Chive Chantilly.* Beat the remaining heavy cream in a medium bowl with an electric mixer on high speed until stiff peaks form. Gently stir in chives. Serve with the soup and sprinkle with the pecans.

Makes 8 servings

Prep Time: 30 minutes
Cook Time: 30 minutes

 Tip

To toast pecans, spread them in a single layer on a jelly-roll pan. Bake at 300°F. for 15 minutes or until the pecans are toasted. Cool and use as directed above.

Sweet Potato & Pecan Soup

Hearty Vegetable Pasta Soup

1 tablespoon vegetable oil

1 small onion, chopped

3 cups reduced-sodium chicken broth

1 can (about 14 ounces) diced tomatoes, undrained

1 medium potato, unpeeled and cubed

2 carrots, sliced

1 stalk celery, sliced

1 teaspoon dried basil

½ teaspoon salt

⅛ teaspoon black pepper

⅓ cup uncooked mini bow-tie pasta

2 ounces fresh spinach, stemmed and chopped

1. Heat oil in large saucepan or Dutch oven over medium-high heat. Add onion; cook and stir until translucent. Add broth, tomatoes with juice, potato, carrots, celery, basil, salt and pepper; bring to a boil over high heat. Reduce heat to medium-low; simmer, uncovered, 20 minutes or until potato and carrots are very tender, stirring occasionally.

2. Stir in pasta; simmer 8 minutes or until pasta is tender.

3. Stir spinach into soup. Simmer 2 minutes or until spinach is wilted. Serve immediately. *Makes 6 servings*

Easy Mushroom Soup

1¾ cups SWANSON® Beef Broth (Regular, 50% Less Sodium *or* Certified Organic)

1¾ cups SWANSON® Chicken Broth (Regular, Natural Goodness® *or* Certified Organic)

⅛ teaspoon ground black pepper

⅛ teaspoon dried rosemary leaves, crushed

8 ounces fresh mushrooms, sliced (about 2 cups)

¼ cup thinly sliced carrots

¼ cup finely chopped onion

¼ cup sliced celery

¼ cup fresh or frozen peas

1 tablespoon sliced green onion

1. Heat the broth, black pepper, rosemary, mushrooms, carrots, onion, celery and peas in a 4-quart saucepan over medium heat to a boil. Reduce the heat to low. Cover and cook for 15 minutes.

2. Add the green onion. Cook for 5 minutes more or until the vegetables are tender.   *Makes 4 servings*

Quick and Zesty Vegetable Soup

1 pound lean ground beef

½ cup chopped onion

Salt and pepper

2 cans (14½ ounces each) DEL MONTE® Stewed Tomatoes - Italian Recipe

2 cans (14 ounces each) beef broth

1 can (14½ ounces) DEL MONTE® Mixed Vegetables

½ cup uncooked medium egg noodles

½ teaspoon dried oregano

1. Brown meat with onion in large pot. Cook until onion is tender; drain. Season to taste with salt and pepper.

2. Stir in remaining ingredients. Bring to boil; reduce heat. Cover and simmer 15 minutes or until noodles are tender.   *Makes 8 servings*

Easy Mushroom Soup

Split Pea Soup

1 package (16 ounces) dried green or yellow split peas

1 pound smoked pork hocks *or* 4 ounces smoked sausage links, sliced and quartered *or* 1 meaty ham bone

7 cups water

1 medium onion, chopped

2 medium carrots, chopped

¾ teaspoon salt

½ teaspoon dried basil

¼ teaspoon dried oregano

¼ teaspoon black pepper

1. Rinse peas thoroughly in colander under cold running water, picking out any debris or blemished peas.

2. Place peas, pork hocks and water in large saucepan or Dutch oven. Add onion, carrots, salt, basil, oregano and pepper; bring to a boil over high heat. Reduce heat to medium-low; simmer, uncovered, 1 hour and 15 minutes or until peas are tender, stirring occasionally. (Stir frequently near end of cooking to keep soup from scorching.)

3. Remove pork hocks; cool. Cut pork into bite-size pieces; set aside. Carefully ladle 3 cups hot soup into food processor or blender; process until smooth.

4. Return puréed soup and pork to saucepan; heat through. (If soup is too thick, add water until desired consistency is reached.)   *Makes 6 servings*

Vegetable Minestrone Soup

2 tablespoons olive or vegetable oil

2 medium zucchini, cut in half lengthwise and thickly sliced (about 3 cups)

2 cloves garlic, minced

½ teaspoon dried rosemary leaves, crushed

4 cups SWANSON® Vegetable Broth (Regular *or* Certified Organic)

1 can (about 14½ ounces) diced tomatoes, drained

1 can (about 19 ounces) white kidney beans (cannellini), rinsed and drained

½ cup uncooked corkscrew-shaped pasta (rotini)

¼ cup grated Parmesan cheese (optional)

1. Heat the oil in a 6-quart saucepot. Add the zucchini, garlic and rosemary and cook until the zucchini is tender-crisp.

2. Stir the broth and tomatoes in the saucepot and heat to a boil. Reduce the heat to low. Cover and cook for 10 minutes.

3. Increase the heat to medium. Stir in the beans and pasta. Cook for 10 minutes or until the pasta is tender. Serve with the cheese, if desired.

Makes 8 servings

Prep Time: 10 minutes
Cook Time: 30 minutes

Beans
& Legumes
* * *

Hearty Bean & Barley Soup

    1 tablespoon olive oil
    2 large carrots, chopped (about 1 cup)
    2 stalks celery, sliced (about 1 cup)
    1 medium onion, chopped (about 1 cup)
 3½ cups SWANSON® Vegetable Broth (Regular *or* Certified Organic)
    1 can (about 15 ounces) red kidney beans, rinsed and drained
    1 can (14½ ounces) diced tomatoes
    ¼ cup uncooked pearl barley
    2 cups firmly packed chopped fresh spinach leaves
      Ground black pepper

1. Heat the oil in a 4-quart saucepan over medium-high heat. Add the carrots, celery and onion. Cook and stir until the vegetables are tender.

2. Stir in the broth, beans, tomatoes and barley. Heat to a boil. Reduce the heat to low. Cover and cook for 30 minutes or until the barley is done.

3. Stir in the spinach and season to taste with black pepper. Cook until the spinach is tender.   *Makes 6 servings*

Prep Time: 15 minutes
Cook Time: 40 minutes

Country Bean Soup

1¼ cups dried navy beans or lima beans, rinsed and drained
2½ cups water
¼ pound salt pork or fully cooked ham, chopped
¼ cup chopped onion
½ teaspoon dried oregano
¼ teaspoon salt
¼ teaspoon ground ginger
¼ teaspoon dried sage
¼ teaspoon black pepper
2 cups milk
2 tablespoons butter

1. Place beans in large saucepan; add enough water to cover. Bring to a boil; reduce heat and simmer 2 minutes. Remove from heat; cover and let stand for 1 hour. (Or, cover beans with water and soak overnight.)

2. Drain beans and return to saucepan. Stir in 2½ cups water, salt pork, onion, oregano, salt, ginger, sage and pepper; bring to a boil. Reduce heat; cover and simmer 2 to 2½ hours or until beans are tender. (If necessary, add more water during cooking.)

3. Add milk and butter, stirring until soup is heated through and butter is melted. Season with additional salt and pepper, if desired.

Makes 6 servings

Veg•All® Black Bean Soup

1 package (14 ounces) smoked sausage, cut into ½-inch slices
2 cans (15 ounces each) VEG•ALL® Original Mixed Vegetables
2 cans (15 ounces each) black beans with spices, drained and rinsed
2 cans (14½ ounces each) chicken broth

In large soup kettle, lightly brown sausage. Add Veg•All, beans and chicken broth; heat until hot. Serve immediately. *Makes 4 to 6 servings*

Country Bean Soup

Smoky Navy Bean Soup

2 tablespoons olive oil, divided
4 ounces Canadian bacon or ham, diced
1 cup diced onion
1 large carrot, thinly sliced
1 stalk celery, thinly sliced
3 cups water
6 ounces red potatoes, diced
2 bay leaves
¼ teaspoon dried tarragon
1 can (about 15 ounces) navy beans, rinsed and drained
1½ teaspoons liquid smoke
½ teaspoon salt
½ teaspoon black pepper

1. Heat 1 tablespoon oil in large saucepan or Dutch oven over medium-high heat. Add Canadian bacon; cook 2 minutes or until brown. Transfer to plate.

2. Add onion, carrot and celery to saucepan; cook and stir 4 minutes or until onion is translucent. Add water; bring to a boil over high heat. Add potatoes, bay leaves and tarragon; return to a boil. Reduce heat; cover and simmer 20 minutes or until potatoes are tender.

3. Stir in beans, bacon, remaining 1 tablespoon oil, liquid smoke, salt and pepper; heat through. Remove and discard bay leaves.   *Makes 6 servings*

Pasta Fagioli

1 jar (1 pound 10 ounces) RAGÚ® Chunky Gardenstyle Pasta Sauce
1 can (19 ounces) white kidney beans, rinsed and drained
1 box (10 ounces) frozen chopped spinach, thawed
8 ounces ditalini pasta, cooked and drained (reserve 2 cups pasta water)

1. In 6-quart saucepot, combine Ragú Pasta Sauce, beans, spinach, pasta and reserved pasta water; heat through.

2. Season, if desired, with salt, ground black pepper and grated Parmesan cheese.
Makes 4 servings

Prep Time: 20 minutes
Cook Time: 10 minutes

Easy Vegetarian Vegetable Bean Soup

3 cans (about 14 ounces each) vegetable broth
2 cups cubed unpeeled potatoes
2 cups sliced leeks, white part only (about 3 medium)
1 can (about 14 ounces) diced tomatoes, undrained
1 medium onion, chopped
1 cup chopped or shredded cabbage
1 cup sliced celery
1 cup sliced carrots
3 cloves garlic, chopped
⅛ teaspoon dried rosemary
1 can (about 15 ounces) white beans, drained
   Salt and black pepper

Slow Cooker Directions

1. Combine broth, potatoes, leeks, tomatoes with juice, onion, cabbage, celery, carrots, garlic and rosemary in 5-quart slow cooker.

2. Cover; cook on LOW 8 hours.

3. Stir in beans; season with salt and pepper. Cover; cook about 30 minutes or until beans are heated through.
Makes 10 servings

Southwestern Chicken & White Bean Soup

1 tablespoon vegetable oil

1 pound skinless, boneless chicken breasts, cut into 1-inch pieces

1¾ cups SWANSON® Chicken Broth (Regular, Natural Goodness™
    or Certified Organic)

1 cup PACE® Chunky Salsa

3 cloves garlic, minced

2 teaspoons ground cumin

1 can (about 16 ounces) small white beans, rinsed and drained

1 cup frozen whole kernel corn

1 large onion, chopped (about 1 cup)

1. Heat the oil in a 10-inch skillet over medium-high heat. Add the chicken and cook until well browned on all sides, stirring often.

2. Stir the broth, salsa, garlic, cumin, beans, corn and onion in a 3½-quart slow cooker. Add the chicken.

3. Cover and cook on LOW for 8 to 10 hours* or until the chicken is cooked through.   *Makes 6 servings*

*Or on HIGH 4 to 5 hours.

Lentil Soup with Ham

3½ cups chicken broth

1 pound ham slice or ham steak, trimmed and cut into bite-size pieces

1 cup (6½ ounces) dried brown lentils, rinsed and drained

1 medium carrot, peeled and diced

½ medium onion, chopped (about ¾ cup)

1 medium jalapeño pepper,* seeded and finely chopped

½ teaspoon dried thyme

*Jalapeño peppers can sting and irritate the skin, so wear rubber gloves when handling peppers and do not touch your eyes.

Combine all ingredients in large saucepan; bring to a boil over high heat. Reduce heat; cover and simmer 30 minutes or until lentils are tender. Let stand, covered, about 15 minutes before serving.   *Makes 4 servings*

Chowders & Bisques

* * *

Chicken and Corn Chowder

 1 tablespoon olive or vegetable oil
 1 pound boneless skinless chicken breasts, cut into ½-inch pieces
 3 cups frozen corn, thawed
 ¾ cup coarsely chopped onion (about 1 medium)
 1 to 2 tablespoons water
 1 cup diced carrots
 2 tablespoons finely chopped jalapeño pepper* (optional)
 ½ teaspoon dried oregano
 ¼ teaspoon dried thyme
 3 cups reduced-sodium chicken broth
1½ cups milk
 ½ teaspoon salt

Jalapeño peppers can sting and irritate the skin, so wear rubber gloves when handling peppers and do not touch your eyes.

1. Heat oil in large saucepan over medium heat. Add chicken; cook and stir about 10 minutes or until browned. Remove from pan; set aside.

2. Add corn and onion to saucepan; cook and stir about 5 minutes or until onion is tender. Place 1 cup corn mixture in food processor or blender; process until finely chopped, adding water to liquify mixture.

3. Add carrots, jalapeño, if desired, oregano and thyme to saucepan; cook and stir about 5 minutes or until corn begins to brown. Return chicken to saucepan with broth, milk, puréed corn mixture and salt; bring to a boil. Reduce heat to low; cover and simmer 15 to 20 minutes.   *Makes 4 servings*

Tomato-Basil Crab Bisque

    1 tablespoon butter
    ½ cup chopped onion
    1 can (8 ounces) HUNT'S® Tomato Sauce with Roasted Garlic
    1 cup half-and-half
    1 cup coarsely chopped cooked crab meat
    ½ cup chicken broth
    ¼ teaspoon salt
    ⅛ teaspoon ground black pepper
    ¼ cup chopped fresh basil leaves

1. Melt butter in a medium saucepan over medium-high heat. Add onion;
cook 3 minutes or until tender, stirring frequently.

2. Add tomato sauce, half-and-half, crab, broth, salt and pepper. Bring just to
a boil; reduce heat to low. Cover tightly and simmer 5 minutes. Sprinkle with
basil before serving.   *Makes 4 servings*

Cheddared Farmhouse Chowder

  1½ cups milk
    1 can (10¾ ounces) condensed cream of mushroom soup, undiluted
    1 bag (16 ounces) frozen corn, carrots and broccoli, thawed
    2 medium baking potatoes, cut into ½-inch cubes
    ½ teaspoon dried thyme
    ¼ teaspoon black pepper
    ⅛ teaspoon ground red pepper (optional)
    ½ cup frozen peas, thawed
    ¼ teaspoon salt
    ¾ cup (3 ounces) shredded sharp Cheddar cheese

1. Combine milk and soup in large saucepan; whisk until well blended.
Bring to a boil over medium-high heat, stirring frequently.

2. Add vegetable mixture, potatoes, thyme, black pepper and ground
red pepper, if desired; bring to a boil. Reduce heat; cover and simmer
15 minutes, stirring frequently. Remove from heat; stir in peas and salt.
Let stand 5 minutes; top with cheese just before serving.   *Makes 4 servings*

Tomato-Basil Crab Bisque

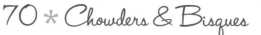

Cream of Broccoli Soup

3 tablespoon butter, divided
3 cups French or rustic Italian bread, cut into ½-inch cubes
1 tablespoon olive oil
¼ cup grated Parmesan cheese
1 large onion, chopped
8 cups (about 1½ pounds) chopped broccoli
3 cups chicken broth
1 cup whipping cream or half-and-half
1½ teaspoons salt
½ teaspoon black pepper

1. Preheat oven to 350°F. Melt 1 tablespoon butter in microwavable bowl; toss with bread cubes and oil until coated. Add cheese; toss to coat. Transfer bread cubes to 15×10-inch jelly-roll pan. Bake 12 to 14 minutes or until golden brown, stirring after 8 minutes. Cool completely.

2. Melt remaining 2 tablespoons butter in large saucepan over medium heat. Add onion; cook 5 minutes, stirring occasionally. Add broccoli and broth; cover and bring to a boil over high heat. Reduce heat; simmer 25 minutes or until broccoli is very tender. Cool 10 minutes.

3. Transfer soup in batches to blender or food processor; blend until smooth. Return to saucepan. Stir in cream, salt and pepper; heat through. *Do not boil.* Top soup with croutons just before serving. *Makes 8 servings*

Note: Soup may be cooled and refrigerated up to 2 days before serving.

Deep Bayou Chowder

1 tablespoon vegetable oil
1½ cups chopped onions
1 large green bell pepper, chopped
1 large carrot, chopped
8 ounces red potatoes, diced
1 cup frozen corn
1 cup water
½ teaspoon dried thyme
2 cups milk
2 tablespoons chopped parsley
1½ teaspoons seafood seasoning
¾ teaspoon salt

1. Heat oil in large saucepan or Dutch oven over medium-high heat. Add onions, pepper and carrot; cook and stir 4 minutes or until onions are translucent.

2. Add potatoes, corn, water and thyme; bring to a boil over high heat. Reduce heat; cover and simmer 15 minutes or until potatoes are tender.

3. Stir in milk, parsley, seasoning and salt; cook 5 minutes.

Makes 6 servings

Tip

Red potatoes are also called boiling potatoes. Their waxy flesh contains more moisture and less starch than russet potatoes, which makes them better suited for boiling than for baking.

Butternut Squash Soup

2 teaspoons olive oil
1 large sweet onion, chopped
1 medium red bell pepper, chopped
2 packages (10 ounces each) frozen puréed butternut squash, thawed
1 can (10¾ ounces) condensed reduced-sodium chicken broth, undiluted
¼ teaspoon ground nutmeg
⅛ teaspoon white pepper
½ cup half-and-half

1. Heat oil in large saucepan over medium-high heat. Add onion and bell pepper; cook 5 minutes, stirring occasionally. Add squash, broth, nutmeg and white pepper; bring to a boil over high heat. Reduce heat; cover and simmer about 15 minutes or until vegetables are very tender.

2. Purée soup in saucepan with hand-held immersion blender. Or, purée soup in batches in food processor or blender. Return soup to saucepan. Stir in half-and-half; heat through. Add water if necessary to thin soup to desired consistency. *Makes 4 servings*

Turkey Chowder

2 potatoes, peeled and cubed
1 (10-ounce) package frozen cut green beans
1½ cups water
2 HERB-OX® chicken flavored instant bouillon cubes
½ teaspoon dried basil leaves
½ teaspoon black pepper
1 tablespoon cornstarch
1½ cups milk
2 cups JENNIE-O TURKEY STORE® Turkey, cooked, cubed

In large saucepan over medium-high heat, combine potatoes, beans, water, bouillon, basil and black pepper. Heat to boiling; reduce heat to low. Cover. Simmer 10 minutes or until potatoes are tender, stirring occasionally. Stir together cornstarch and milk. Stir into potato mixture. Cook and stir over medium-high heat 5 minutes or until thickened. Stir in turkey. Cook 2 minutes or until thoroughly heated. *Makes 6 servings*

Butternut Squash Soup

Shrimp and Pepper Bisque

 1 bag (12 ounces) frozen stir-fry-style mixed peppers and vegetables,
    thawed
½ pound frozen cauliflower florets, thawed
 1 medium stalk celery, sliced
 1 can (about 14 ounces) reduced-sodium chicken broth
 1 tablespoon seafood seasoning
½ teaspoon dried thyme
12 ounces medium raw shrimp, peeled
 2 cups half-and-half
 2 to 3 green onions, finely chopped

Slow Cooker Directions

1. Combine stir-fry mix, cauliflower, celery, broth, seafood seasoning and thyme in 3½ to 4-quart slow cooker. Cover; cook on LOW 8 hours or on HIGH 4 hours.

2. Stir in shrimp. Cover; cook 15 minutes or until pink and opaque.

3. Transfer soup in batches to blender or food processor; blend until smooth. Return to slow cooker. Stir in half-and-half; heat through. Sprinkle with green onions before serving.   *Makes 4 servings*

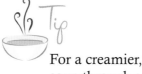

For a creamier, smoother consistency, strain the soup through several layers of damp cheesecloth.

Shrimp and Pepper Bisque

Chilis
& Gumbos
* * *

Hearty Chicken Chili

1 medium onion, finely chopped

1 small jalapeño pepper,* seeded and minced

1 clove garlic, minced

1½ teaspoons chili powder

¾ teaspoon salt

½ teaspoon black pepper

½ teaspoon ground cumin

½ teaspoon dried oregano

¼ teaspoon red pepper flakes (optional)

1½ pounds boneless skinless chicken thighs, cut into 1-inch pieces

2 cans (about 15 ounces each) hominy, rinsed and drained

1 can (about 15 ounces) pinto beans, rinsed and drained

1 cup chicken broth

1 tablespoon all-purpose flour (optional)

Chopped fresh parsley or fresh cilantro (optional)

Jalapeño peppers can sting and irritate the skin, so wear rubber gloves when handling peppers and do not touch your eyes.

Slow Cooker Directions

1. Combine onion, jalapeño, garlic, chili powder, salt, black pepper, cumin, oregano and red pepper flakes, if desired, in slow cooker.

2. Stir in chicken, hominy, beans and broth. Cover; cook on LOW 7 hours.

3. If thicker chili is desired, combine 1 tablespoon flour and 3 tablespoons cooking liquid in small bowl; add to slow cooker. Cover; cook on HIGH 10 minutes or until thickened. Garnish with parsley.   *Makes 6 servings*

Texas Chili

2 tablespoons vegetable oil

3½ pounds beef top round steak, ¾ inch thick, cut into ¼-inch pieces

3 medium onions, chopped (about 1½ cups)

2 medium green peppers, chopped (about 1 cup)

2 cloves garlic, minced or 1 teaspoon garlic powder

4 cups V8® 100% Vegetable Juice

3 tablespoons chili powder

¼ teaspoon ground red pepper

1 can (14½ ounces) diced tomatoes

1. Heat **1 tablespoon** of the oil in a 6-quart saucepot over medium-high heat. Add the beef in 3 batches and cook until well browned. Remove the beef with a slotted spoon and set aside. Pour off any fat.

2. Reduce the heat to medium and add the remaining oil. Add the onions, green peppers and garlic. Cook and stir until the vegetables are tender-crisp. Pour off any fat.

3. Add the vegetable juice, chili powder, red pepper and tomatoes. Heat to a boil. Reduce the heat to low and return the beef to the saucepot. Cover and cook for 1 hour and 45 minutes or until beef is fork-tender.

Makes 8 servings

Start to Finish Time: 2 hours 40 minutes
Hands on Time: 30 minutes
Cook Time: 2 hours 10 minutes

Chicken Gumbo Ya-Ya

¼ cup all-purpose flour
1 teaspoon dried thyme leaves, crushed
1¾ pounds skinless, boneless chicken thighs, cut into 1-inch pieces
2 tablespoons vegetable oil
1 pound smoked sausage, cut into 1-inch pieces
1 can (10¾ ounces) CAMPBELL'S® Condensed Cream of Celery Soup
   (Regular *or* 98% Fat Free)
1 can (10½ ounces) CAMPBELL'S® Condensed Chicken Broth
1 can (about 14½ ounces) diced tomatoes
2 teaspoons hot pepper sauce
1 large onion, chopped (about 1 cup)
1 large green pepper, chopped (about 1 cup)
3 stalks celery, sliced (about 1½ cups)
2 bay leaves
1 package (10 ounces) frozen cut okra, thawed
   Hot cooked rice (optional)

1. Mix the flour and thyme in a gallon-size resealable plastic bag. Add the chicken and shake to coat.

2. Heat the oil in a 12-inch skillet over medium-high heat. Add the chicken and cook until well browned, stirring often. Remove the chicken from the skillet. Add the sausage to the skillet and cook until well browned, stirring often.

3. Stir the chicken, sausage, soup, broth, tomatoes, hot pepper sauce, onion, green pepper, celery, bay leaves and okra in a 6-quart slow cooker.

4. Cover and cook on LOW for 8 to 9 hours* or until the chicken is cooked through. Remove the bay leaves. Serve with the rice, if desired.

Makes 8 servings

Or on HIGH for 4 to 5 hours.

Kitchen Tip: You can also stir ½ **pound** of cooked medium shrimp in the cooker during the last 30 minutes of cooking.

Prep Time: 20 minutes
Cook Time: 8 hours

Chicken Gumbo Ya-Ya

Simple Turkey Chili

1 pound ground turkey

1 small onion, chopped

1 can (28 ounces) diced tomatoes, undrained

1 can (about 15 ounces) black beans, rinsed and drained

1 can (about 15 ounces) chickpeas, rinsed and drained

1 can (about 15 ounces) kidney beans, rinsed and drained

1 can (8 ounces) tomato sauce

1 can (4 ounces) chopped mild green chilies

1 to 2 tablespoons chili powder

1. Cook turkey and onion in large saucepan or Dutch oven over medium-high heat until turkey is cooked through, stirring to break up meat. Drain fat.

2. Stir in remaining ingredients; bring to a boil. Reduce heat and simmer, stirring occasionally, about 20 minutes. *Makes 8 servings*

Serving Suggestion: Serve the chili over split baked potatoes.

Jiffy Chicken & Rice Gumbo

1 (6.9-ounce) package RICE-A-RONI® Chicken Flavor

1 small green bell pepper, coarsely chopped

2 tablespoons margarine or butter

1 pound boneless, skinless chicken breasts, cut into 1-inch pieces

1 (14½-ounce) can diced tomatoes with garlic and onion, undrained

¾ to 1 teaspoon Creole or Cajun seasoning*

½ teaspoon cayenne pepper, ¼ teaspoon dried oregano and ¼ teaspoon dried thyme can be substituted.

1. In large skillet over medium heat, sauté rice-vermicelli mix and bell pepper with margarine until vermicelli is golden brown.

2. Slowly stir in 2¼ cups water, chicken, tomatoes, Creole seasoning and Special Seasonings; bring to a boil. Reduce heat to low. Cover; simmer 15 to 20 minutes or until rice is tender. *Makes 4 servings*

Prep Time: 5 minutes
Cook Time: 30 minutes

Simple Turkey Chili

Quick Ranchero Chili

    1 pound ground beef
    1 medium onion, chopped (about ½ cup)
    2 tablespoons chili powder
    1 can (10¾ ounces) CAMPBELL'S® Condensed Creamy Ranchero
        Tomato Soup
    ½ cup water
    1 can (about 15 ounces) small red beans *or* red kidney beans, rinsed and
        drained
        Shredded Cheddar cheese

1. Cook the beef, onion and chili powder in a 10-inch skillet over medium-high heat until the beef is well browned, stirring frequently to break up the meat. Pour off any fat.

2. Stir in the soup, water and beans and heat to a boil.

3. Cover and reduce the heat to low. Cook for 10 minutes. Top with the cheese.   *Makes 4 servings*

Shrimp Gumbo

    1 package (16 ounces) frozen cut okra
    1 can (about 14 ounces) stewed tomatoes, undrained
    2 cups water
    ½ pound cooked ham or sausage, diced
    1 can (8 ounces) tomato sauce
    2 medium onions, sliced
    2 tablespoons vegetable oil
    ½ teaspoon red pepper flakes
    1 bay leaf
        Salt and black pepper
    2 pounds frozen large raw shrimp, peeled and deveined

Combine all ingredients except shrimp in large saucepan. Bring to a boil over high heat. Reduce heat to low; simmer, partially covered, 30 minutes. Stir in shrimp. Cook, partially covered, 10 to 15 minutes or until shrimp are pink and opaque, stirring occasionally. Remove bay leaf.   *Makes 6 servings*

Quick Ranchero Chili

Confetti Chicken Chili

1 pound ground chicken or turkey

1 large onion, chopped

2 cans (about 14 ounces each) reduced-sodium chicken broth

1 can (about 15 ounces) Great Northern beans, rinsed and drained

2 carrots, chopped

1 medium green bell pepper, chopped

2 plum tomatoes, chopped

1 jalapeño pepper,* finely chopped (optional)

2 teaspoons chili powder

½ teaspoon ground red pepper

Jalapeño peppers can sting and irritate the skin, so wear rubber gloves when handling peppers and do not touch your eyes.

1. Cook chicken and onion in large nonstick saucepan over medium heat 5 minutes or until chicken is browned, stirring to break up meat. Drain fat.

2. Add broth, beans, carrots, bell pepper, tomatoes, jalapeño, if desired, chili powder and ground red pepper; bring to a boil. Reduce heat to low; simmer 15 minutes. *Makes 4 to 6 servings*

Veg•All® Gumbo

1 teaspoon canola oil

½ cup chopped celery

½ cup chopped white onion

¼ cup chopped green pepper

1 pound skinless, boneless chicken breasts, cubed

½ pound ground turkey sausage

1 can (15 ounces) VEG•ALL® Original Mixed Vegetables, drained

1 can (14½ ounces) diced tomatoes, undrained

In medium fry pan, heat oil over medium-high heat; sauté celery, onion, green pepper, cubed chicken and sausage 5 minutes or until cooked. Stir in Veg•All and tomatoes; cook until heated through. *Makes 8 servings*

Confetti Chicken Chili

Chunky Beef Chili

1½ pounds beef for stew, cut into 1 to 1½-inch pieces
2 tablespoons vegetable oil
  Salt
1 medium onion, chopped
1 medium jalapeño pepper, minced (with seeds)
2 cans (14½ ounces each) chili-seasoned diced tomatoes

1. Heat 1 tablespoon oil in stockpot over medium heat until hot. Brown ½ of beef; remove from stockpot. Repeat with remaining beef. Remove beef from stockpot. Season with salt, as desired.

2. Add remaining 1 tablespoon oil, onion and jalapeño pepper to stockpot. Cook and stir 5 to 8 minutes or until vegetables are tender. Return beef and juices to stockpot. Add tomatoes; bring to a boil. Reduce heat; cover tightly and simmer 1¾ to 2¼ hours or until beef is fork-tender.   *Makes 4 servings*

Cook's Tip: Canned Mexican or Southwest-style diced tomatoes may be substituted for chili-seasoned tomatoes.

Prep and Cook Time: 2 to 2¾ hours

Favorite recipe courtesy of *The Beef Checkoff*

Weeknight Chili

1 pound ground beef or turkey
1 package (1¼ ounces) chili seasoning mix
1 can (about 15 ounces) red kidney beans, rinsed and drained
1 can (about 14 ounces) diced tomatoes with green chiles, undrained
1 can (8 ounces) tomato sauce
1 cup (4 ounces) shredded Cheddar cheese
  Sliced green onions (optional)

Slow Cooker Directions
1. Brown beef in large skillet over medium-high heat, stirring to break up meat. Drain fat. Stir in seasoning mix.

2. Place beef mixture, beans, tomatoes with juice and tomato sauce in slow cooker. Cover; cook on LOW 4 to 6 hours. Top each serving with cheese; garnish with green onions.   *Makes 4 servings*

The publisher would like to thank the companies and organizations listed below for the use of their recipes and photographs in this publication.

Courtesy of The Beef Checkoff

Campbell Soup Company

ConAgra Foods, Inc.

Delmarva Poultry Industry, Inc.

Del Monte Corporation

The Golden Grain Company®

Hormel Foods, LLC

Jennie-O Turkey Store, LLC

VELVEETA is a registered trademark of Kraft Foods

Reckitt Benckiser Inc.

Riviana Foods Inc.

Unilever

Veg•All®

Barley
Greens, White Bean and Barley Soup, 38
Hearty Bean & Barley Soup, 56
Hearty Mushroom Barley Soup, 44
Beans
Confetti Chicken Chili, 88
Country Bean Soup, 58
Easy Vegetarian Vegetable Bean Soup, 62
Grandma Ruth's Minestrone, 10
Greens, White Bean and Barley Soup, 38
Hearty Bean & Barley Soup, 56
Hearty Chicken Chili, 78
Homestyle Ham & Bean Soup, 14
Pasta Fagioli, 62
Quick Ranchero Chili, 86
Simple Turkey Chili, 84
Smoky Navy Bean Soup, 60
Southwestern Chicken & White Bean Soup, 64
Turkey Chowder, 74
Veg•All® Black Bean Soup, 58
Vegetable Minestrone Soup, 54
Weeknight Chili, 90
Beef *(see also* **Beef, Ground***)*
Beef and Beet Borscht, 18
Beef, Lentil and Onion Soup, 16
Chunky Beef Chili, 90
Meatball & Pasta Soup, 12
1-2-3 Steak Soup, 15
Texas Chili, 80
Beef, Ground
Beefy Broccoli & Cheese Soup, 6
Grandma Ruth's Minestrone, 10
Kansas City Steak Soup, 12
Lasagna-Style Soup, 14
Quick and Zesty Vegetable Soup, 50
Quick Ranchero Chili, 86
Weeknight Chili, 90
Beefy Broccoli & Cheese Soup, 6
Butternut Squash Soup, 74

Cabbage
Easy Vegetarian Vegetable Bean Soup, 62
Grandma Ruth's Minestrone, 10
Ham, Potato & Cabbage Soup, 8
Kielbasa & Cabbage Soup, 18
Cheddared Farmhouse Chowder, 68
Cheesy Spinach Soup, 36
Chicken
Chicken and Corn Chowder, 66
Chicken & Herb Dumplings, 24
Chicken and Wild Rice Soup, 26

Chicken Gumbo Ya-Ya, 82
Chicken Tortellini Soup, 32
Chunky Chicken Vegetable Soup, 29
Confetti Chicken Chili, 88
Creamy Chicken Tortilla Soup, 34
Hearty Chicken Chili, 78
Jiffy Chicken & Rice Gumbo, 84
Shaker Chicken and Noodle Soup, 28
Southwestern Chicken & White Bean Soup, 64
Spaghetti Soup, 20
Veg•All® Gumbo, 88
Chunky Beef Chili, 90
Chunky Chicken Vegetable Soup, 29
Confetti Chicken Chili, 88
Country Bean Soup, 58
Country Turkey and Veggie Soup, 22
Cream of Broccoli Soup, 70
Creamy Chicken Tortilla Soup, 34

Deep Bayou Chowder, 72

Easy Mushroom Soup, 50
Easy Vegetarian Vegetable Bean Soup, 62

Grandma Ruth's Minestrone, 10
Greens, White Bean and Barley Soup, 38

Ham, Potato & Cabbage Soup, 8
Hearty Bean & Barley Soup, 56
Hearty Chicken Chili, 78
Hearty Mushroom Barley Soup, 44
Hearty Vegetable Pasta Soup, 48
Homestyle Ham & Bean Soup, 14

Jiffy Chicken & Rice Gumbo, 84

Kansas City Steak Soup, 12
Kielbasa & Cabbage Soup, 18

Lasagna-Style Soup, 14
Lentil Soup with Ham, 64

Meatball & Pasta Soup, 12
Mushrooms
Chicken and Wild Rice Soup, 26
Country Turkey and Veggie Soup, 22
Easy Mushroom Soup, 50
Greens, White Bean and Barley Soup, 38
Hearty Mushroom Barley Soup, 44
1-2-3 Steak Soup, 15

1-2-3 Steak Soup, 15

Pasta
Chicken Tortellini Soup, 32
Country Turkey and Veggie Soup, 22
Grandma Ruth's Minestrone, 10
Hearty Vegetable Pasta Soup, 48
Lasagna-Style Soup, 14
Meatball & Pasta Soup, 12
Pasta Fagioli, 62
Quick and Zesty Vegetable Soup, 50
Rich and Hearty Drumstick Soup, 30
Shaker Chicken and Noodle Soup, 28
Spaghetti Soup, 20
Vegetable Minestrone Soup, 54

Pork (see also **Sausage**)
Country Bean Soup, 58
Ham, Potato & Cabbage Soup, 8
Homestyle Ham & Bean Soup, 14
Lentil Soup with Ham, 64
Shrimp Gumbo, 86
Smoky Navy Bean Soup, 60
Split Pea Soup, 52

Potatoes
Butternut Squash Soup, 74
Cheddared Farmhouse Chowder, 68
Deep Bayou Chowder, 72
Easy Vegetarian Vegetable Bean Soup, 62
Ham, Potato & Cabbage Soup, 8
Hearty Vegetable Pasta Soup, 48
Smoky Navy Bean Soup, 60
Sweet Potato & Pecan Soup, 46
Twice-Baked Potato Soup, 42

Quick and Zesty Vegetable Soup, 50
Quick Ranchero Chili, 86

Rice
Chicken and Wild Rice Soup, 26
Chunky Chicken Vegetable Soup, 29
Jiffy Chicken & Rice Gumbo, 84
Turkey and Rice Soup, 28
Rich and Hearty Drumstick Soup, 30

Sausage
Chicken Gumbo Ya-Ya, 82
Kielbasa & Cabbage Soup, 18
Lasagna-Style Soup, 14
Veg•All® Black Bean Soup, 58
Veg•All® Gumbo, 88

Seafood
Shrimp and Pepper Bisque, 76
Shrimp Gumbo, 86
Tomato-Basil Crab Bisque, 68
Shaker Chicken and Noodle Soup, 28

Shrimp and Pepper Bisque, 76
Shrimp Gumbo, 86
Simple Turkey Chili, 84
Slow Cooker Recipes
Beef, Lentil and Onion Soup, 16
Chicken & Herb Dumplings, 24
Chicken Gumbo Ya-Ya, 82
Country Turkey and Veggie Soup, 22
Creamy Chicken Tortilla Soup, 34
Easy Vegetarian Vegetable Bean Soup, 62
Grandma Ruth's Minestrone, 10
Hearty Chicken Chili, 78
Rich and Hearty Drumstick Soup, 30
Shrimp and Pepper Bisque, 76
Southwestern Chicken & White Bean Soup, 64
Weeknight Chili, 90
Smoky Navy Bean Soup, 60
Southwestern Chicken & White Bean Soup, 64
Spaghetti Soup, 20

Spinach
Cheesy Spinach Soup, 36
Hearty Bean & Barley Soup, 56
Hearty Vegetable Pasta Soup, 48
Meatball & Pasta Soup, 12
Pasta Fagioli, 62
Split Pea Soup, 52
Sweet Potato & Pecan Soup, 46

Texas Chili, 80
Tomato-Basil Crab Bisque, 68
Tomato Soup, 40
Turkey
Country Turkey and Veggie Soup, 22
Rich and Hearty Drumstick Soup, 30
Simple Turkey Chili, 84
Turkey and Rice Soup, 28
Turkey Chowder, 74
Twice-Baked Potato Soup, 42

Veg•All® Black Bean Soup, 58
Veg•All® Gumbo, 88
Vegetable Minestrone Soup, 54

Weeknight Chili, 90

VOLUME MEASUREMENTS (dry)

1/8 teaspoon = 0.5 mL
1/4 teaspoon = 1 mL
1/2 teaspoon = 2 mL
3/4 teaspoon = 4 mL
1 teaspoon = 5 mL
1 tablespoon = 15 mL
2 tablespoons = 30 mL
1/4 cup = 60 mL
1/3 cup = 75 mL
1/2 cup = 125 mL
2/3 cup = 150 mL
3/4 cup = 175 mL
1 cup = 250 mL
2 cups = 1 pint = 500 mL
3 cups = 750 mL
4 cups = 1 quart = 1 L

VOLUME MEASUREMENTS (fluid)

1 fluid ounce (2 tablespoons) = 30 mL
4 fluid ounces (1/2 cup) = 125 mL
8 fluid ounces (1 cup) = 250 mL
12 fluid ounces (1 1/2 cups) = 375 mL
16 fluid ounces (2 cups) = 500 mL

WEIGHTS (mass)

1/2 ounce = 15 g
1 ounce = 30 g
3 ounces = 90 g
4 ounces = 120 g
8 ounces = 225 g
10 ounces = 285 g
12 ounces = 360 g
16 ounces = 1 pound = 450 g

DIMENSIONS

1/16 inch = 2 mm
1/8 inch = 3 mm
1/4 inch = 6 mm
1/2 inch = 1.5 cm
3/4 inch = 2 cm
1 inch = 2.5 cm

OVEN TEMPERATURES

250°F = 120°C
275°F = 140°C
300°F = 150°C
325°F = 160°C
350°F = 180°C
375°F = 190°C
400°F = 200°C
425°F = 220°C
450°F = 230°C

BAKING PAN SIZES

Utensil	Size in Inches/Quarts	Metric Volume	Size in Centimeters
Baking or Cake Pan (square or rectangular)	8×8×2	2 L	20×20×5
	9×9×2	2.5 L	23×23×5
	12×8×2	3 L	30×20×5
	13×9×2	3.5 L	33×23×5
Loaf Pan	8×4×3	1.5 L	20×10×7
	9×5×3	2 L	23×13×7
Round Layer Cake Pan	8×1½	1.2 L	20×4
	9×1½	1.5 L	23×4
Pie Plate	8×1¼	750 mL	20×3
	9×1¼	1 L	23×3
Baking Dish or Casserole	1 quart	1 L	—
	1½ quart	1.5 L	—
	2 quart	2 L	—